TAKING FLIGHT

HOLOCAUST MUSEUM HOUSTON REMEMBERS THE 1.5 MILLION CHILDREN WHO PERISHED IN THE HOLOCAUST

HOLOCAUST MUSEUM HOUSTON
20 YEARS · OF HOPE

ISBN: 978-0-9773988-4-6
10 9 8 7 6 5 4 3 2 1
Printed in Canada.

We at Bernstein Private Wealth Management are truly honored to be a part of an undertaking as meaningful, inspiring and profoundly educational as The Butterfly Project. The adage "those who do not learn from history are doomed to repeat it," is a guiding principle for us at Bernstein, in both our professional and philanthropic activities. Our firm and its employees have a long history of supporting organizations that advance Holocaust remembrance and education, including the effort to create the United States Holocaust Memorial Museum in Washington, D.C. more than 22 years ago. When we first heard of The Butterfly Project from Holocaust Museum Houston, we knew instantly that this was something our firm must support. The ability of The Butterfly Project to find and capture such beauty, while simultaneously honoring the lives of the more than 1.5 million children lost in the tragedy of the Holocaust, is breathtaking and inspiring. At Bernstein, we strive to bring relentless ingenuity to everything we do for our clients and the community. The Butterfly Project embodies this spirit and all the values we hold dear in our quest to build a better society.

On a personal note, several years ago I discovered that during the Holocaust, my grandparents led an effort to bring a group of children to safety in the United States. In early 1939, my grandparents capped months of meticulous planning with a brave trip from their home in Philadelphia to Nazi Germany to convince the German government to grant passage to America for as many children as possible. Miraculously, they were able to rescue 50 children, the single largest group of children brought from the Nazi-occupied region to the United States during the Holocaust. The story was recently made into an HBO documentary, *50 Children — The Rescue Mission of Mr. and Mrs. Kraus* as well as a book of the same name.

The Butterfly Project, with its splendor, beauty and celebration of children, truly speaks to me personally and to our firm. Thank you for letting us be a part of this inspiring project.

Peter Kraus
Chairman and CEO, AB

BERNSTEIN

ACKNOWLEDGMENTS

The magnitude of this project, which spanned more than 1.5 million butterflies and more than twenty years, prevents us from individually recognizing everyone who contributed butterflies, time, donations, wisdom or support. This, however, in no way diminishes our appreciation and our tremendous debt to the many contributors.

We also cannot individually thank those who participated as part of a class project at thousands of elementary, middle and high schools around the world. We express our gratitude to all of the students and teachers who responded to the call of The Butterfly Project and poured their enthusiasm into creating magnificent and moving butterflies.

Holocaust Museum Houston Chair Gail Klein and The Butterfly Project Chair Tali Blumrosen committed to the preservation of the butterflies and the creation of this book in 2014. This publication has now become a reality through the coordination of HMH Trustee Benjamin Warren and the generous sponsorship of Peter Kraus and Bernstein Private Wealth Management. Mr. Kraus's commitment celebrates the lifesaving work of his grandparents, who courageously saved fifty children from Nazi-occupied Europe in 1939.

The HMH Board of Trustees blessed us with their counsel and guidance throughout the lifetime of the project.

Volunteers served as the heart of this undertaking. We thank the many volunteers who served quietly and anonymously.

We acknowledge the efforts of Cyndy Elliot, Susan Myers, and Mary Kay Porter in initiating the project. We also thank current and former HMH staff for their efforts to communicate, educate and support the development of The Butterfly Project and *Taking Flight*. We would like to make special mention of Dr. Kelly J. Zúñiga, Dr. Mary Lee Webeck, Ira Perry and Tamara Savage for their direction and support. Lastly, this book could not have come to completion without the creative efforts of Janice Adamson, Susan Bischoff, Ellen Cregan, Donna Giles, William Johnson, Michael Marvins and Christine Miles.

Holocaust Museum Houston extends sincerest thanks to all supporters for keeping the memory of 1.5 million children alive and for allowing future generations to learn lessons of great magnitude from the Holocaust.

The Butterfly

The last, the very last,
So richly, brightly, dazzlingly yellow.
Perhaps if the sun's tears would sing
against a white stone....

Such, such a yellow
Is carried lightly 'way up high.
It went away I'm sure because it wished to
kiss the world good-bye.

For seven weeks I've lived in here,
Penned up inside this ghetto.
But I have found what I love here.
The dandelions call to me
And the white chestnut branches in the court.
Only I never saw another butterfly.

That butterfly was the last one.
Butterflies don't live here,
in the ghetto.

Pavel Friedmann, June 4, 1942

INTRODUCTION

The last, the very last,
So richly, brightly, dazzlingly yellow.

Exquisite and elusive, the beauty of butterflies taking flight and floating freely has fired the imaginations of children and adults throughout time. From crawling earthbound caterpillar to winged wonder, the butterfly has also long embodied transcendence and transformation. In some cultures, the butterfly symbolizes the soul, and in others, it specifically symbolizes the souls of children.

In 1964, the butterfly took on new significance with the publication of a poem by Pavel Friedmann, a young Czech who wrote while in the Terezin Concentration Camp and ultimately died in Auschwitz in 1944. In a few poignant lines, "The Butterfly" voiced the spirit of the 1.5 million promising children who perished in the Holocaust.

Perhaps if the sun's tears would sing
against a white stone....

Children were especially vulnerable during the Holocaust. Nazi policy advocated killing children of unwanted or dangerous groups, either as part of the racial struggle or as a measure of preventative security. Between 1939 and 1945, the Nazis and their collaborators caused the deaths of as many as 1.5 million children. This number included more than a million Jewish children, tens of thousands of Romani (Gypsy) children and children with physical and mental disabilities.

Such, such a yellow
Is carried lightly 'way up high.
It went away I'm sure because it wished to
kiss the world good-bye.

The poem captured the tragedy of loss and fired the imagination of readers worldwide. In 1995, it inspired staff and supporters of Holocaust Museum Houston (HMH) to launch The Butterfly Project. HMH designed The Butterfly Project to connect a new generation of children to the children who perished in the Nazi era. Three educators designed activities and lesson plans to convey to students the enormity of the loss of innocent life.

Students learned about the experiences of children during the Holocaust through the study of poems and artwork created by children imprisoned in the Czech town of Terezin. Maintained by the Nazis as a "model ghetto" and transfer point, it later came to be known as the German concentration camp Theresienstadt.

A key resource for this project was Hana Volakova's edited collection *I Never Saw Another Butterfly: Children's Drawings and Poems from Terezin Concentration Camp 1942–1944*. The book contains Pavel Friedmann's poem and other children's works that somehow survived and came to light after the war.

Few children survived Theresienstadt or any other camp. To demonstrate this random and pervasive loss of life, teachers walked students through a special butterfly project. Students would receive the name of a child from the Holocaust era and then create a butterfly to commemorate that child and his or her life. Filling the rooms with beauty and color, the butterflies were often suspended from the classroom ceiling. Over a period of time, seemingly at random, teachers would remove a butterfly to represent a child who had perished. Students would return to the classrooms day after day to see if "their" butterfly had survived or perished. Finding that their butterfly had disappeared, the students were shocked, saddened and frequently angry when they learned the fate of the child with whom they had come to identify.

Word of The Butterfly Project spread through the efforts of the Museum and by word of mouth from students and teachers. Students made butterflies of all sizes and dimensions from every available medium. They wrote poetry and letters and created newsletters and journals. They also wrote scripts for plays and videos in which they performed.

For seven weeks I've lived in here,
Penned up inside this ghetto.

Lili Rosenberg, celebrating her eighth birthday in a butterfly costume, serves as an iconic face of innocence for the 1.5 million children who perished in the Holocaust. Lili was the aunt of Holocaust Museum Houston Board Member Gail Danziger Klein.

A poem by a middle school student typifies the response of students to the emotions encountered through the study of the Holocaust and through their participation in The Butterfly Project.

For the Children of Terezin

Inspired by *I Never Saw Another Butterfly: Children's Drawings and Poems from Terezin Concentration Camp 1942–1944*

Those Jewish Children
Who passed through Terezin
Who went through hell
Who lived life—
Not wanting to die
But determined to live—
Have given me hope.

If mere children
If mere children can live every day
Fearing they would not live to see the next,
I can certainly bear my burdens.

Does anyone still weep for these people
After 60 years?
Yes someone does
Yes.

Because I weep now.

My plights will never compare to theirs,
So I cannot give in
Because someone says I should!

I refuse to let my eyes leak for my loss of
Childhood,
Love,
And life,
Because I can still get it all back.

So if those children can die
And still defeat death
Then by God—
I WILL pass this test.

Middle School Student
January 23, 2013

Teachers began sending packages of their students' handmade butterflies to HMH. As momentum grew, packages poured into the Museum daily, but it was not only schools that contributed.

The Butterfly Project had found a deep resonance, stirring creativity and compassion around the world. HMH became known as the institution that was collecting all of these beautiful butterflies, each representing the innocent life of a child.

With that, the project caught fire.

Butterflies began to arrive at the Museum from groups of all ages and descriptions as an outpouring of emotion and remembrance. Day care centers, Girl Scouts, Camp Fire Girls, businesses and corporations, individuals, hospitals, retirement communities, faith-based groups, anti-genocide groups, art clubs and sewing guilds all participated. A group of felt artists in Germany submitted beautiful felted butterflies along with this message: "We created these butterflies in response to the rise of antisemitism we see now in Europe."

Butterflies arrived from Africa, Asia, Australia, North America, South America and Europe as the project inspired people around the globe.

One butterfly even arrived from space. American Astronaut Rex Walheim participated in The Butterfly Project in July 2011 while aboard the final mission of Space Shuttle Atlantis. He created his butterfly in memory of the children who perished in the Holocaust and in honor of Israeli Astronaut Ilan Ramon, who died tragically with six other crew members during the re-entry of Space Shuttle Columbia in February 2003.

But I have found what I love here.

The dandelions call to me

And the white chestnut branches in the court.

Over the course of twenty years, The Butterfly Project has fired the imagination of millions of people and has resulted in the creation of more than 1.5 million stunning butterflies, handmade in every conceivable material, color and form.

And now the time has come for HMH to share the butterflies with the public. While traveling and other exhibits are planned, the Museum also has decided to publish a book to reach the broadest possible audience.

In an action as symbolic as the project, photographs of only 100 butterflies — a fraction of the 1.5 million butterflies received — appear in this book. Those that have alighted on these pages are as individual as their creators and the children they symbolize. Each commemorates a child who perished — often without a grave or headstone — and as such is as anonymous as the child it commemorates. However, we believe that The Butterfly Project has added much more significance to their lives. As Aharon Appelfeld wrote, "Art constantly challenges the process by which an individual person is reduced to anonymity."

Our hope is that this book will not only serve as a commemoration to the children who perished in the Holocaust, but also serve as a challenge to the persistent threat of genocide that continues to confront civilization. As Nicholas Stargardt wrote, "Children were neither just the mute and traumatized witnesses to this war, nor merely its innocent victims; the war invaded their imaginations and the war raged inside them."

Only I never saw another butterfly.

That butterfly was the last one.
Butterflies don't live here, in the ghetto.

Holocaust Museum Houston is honored to share *Taking Flight*. As a middle school student wrote, "I want to honor every child killed, even with my one butterfly....The only way to stop such atrocities from happening again is to teach future doctors, lawyers, teachers and ambassadors and so on and so forth....I want to make a difference in the world one butterfly at a time."

"Remember us, for we were the children whose dreams and lives were stolen away."

~ BARBARA SONEK

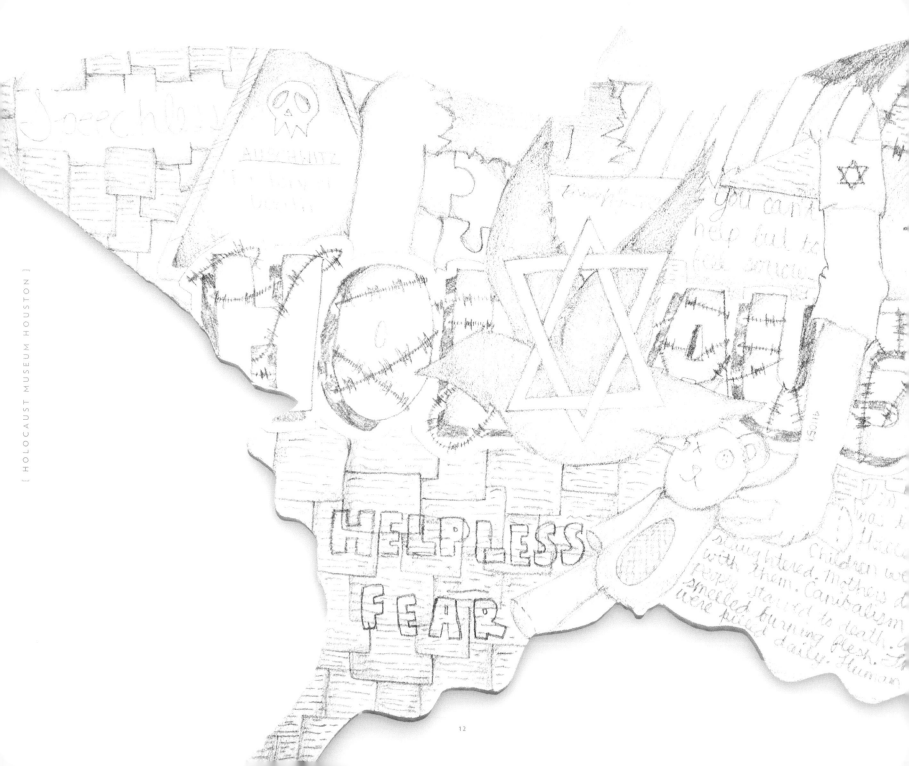

REMINGTON 2009

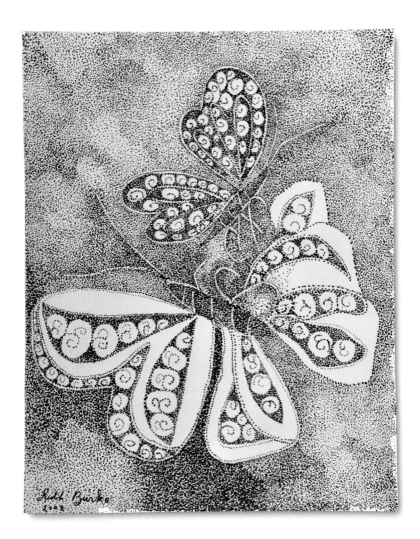

Y. Zaddik

For Whom
the
Bell Tolls

21

22

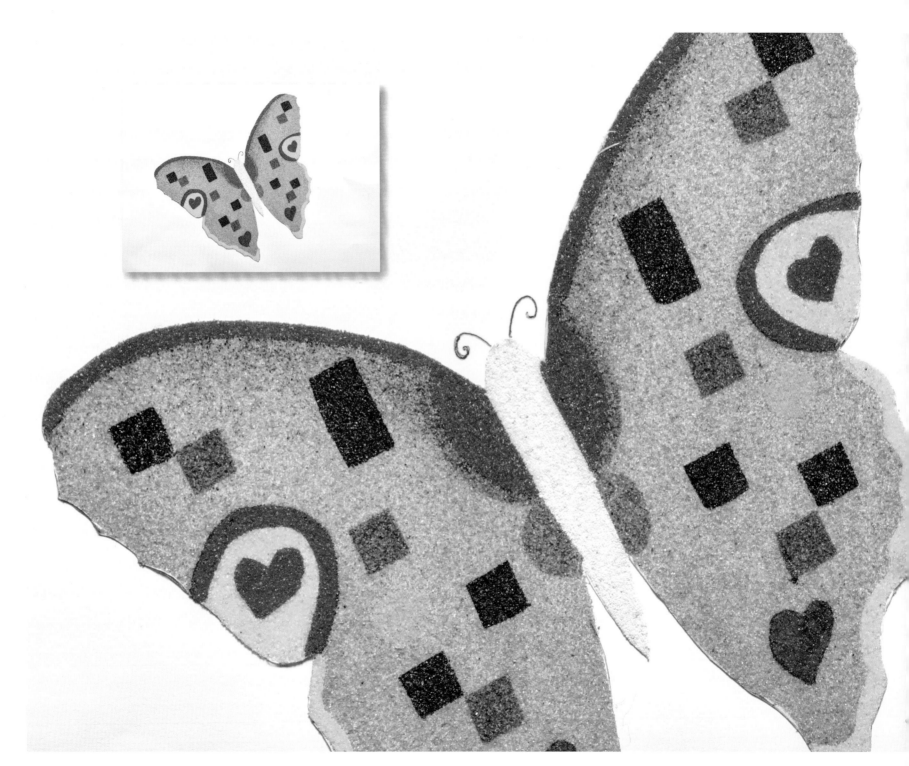

A·P   Not Even Tryin

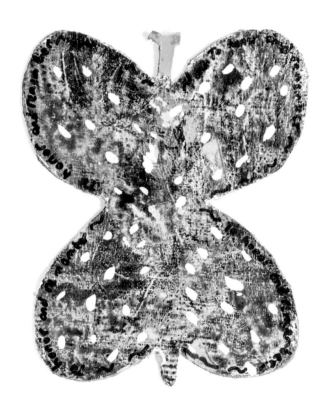

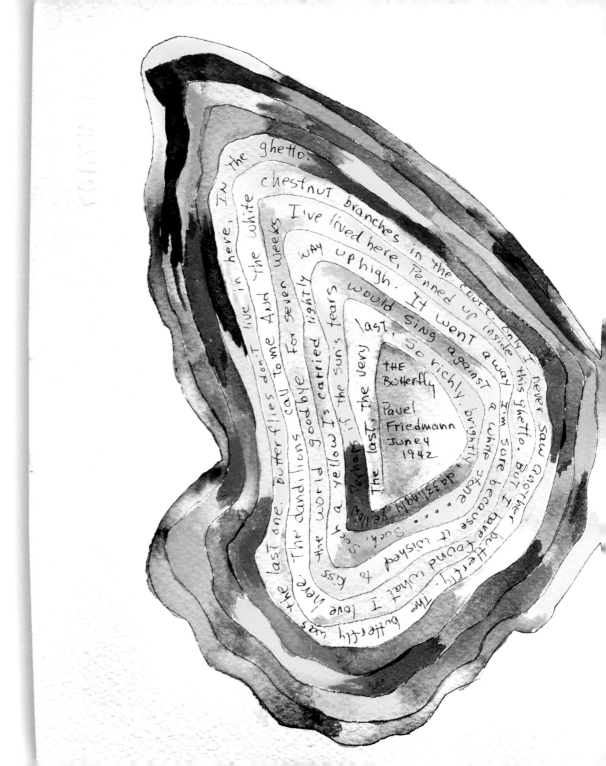

In the ghetto. In the ghetto. I never saw another
chestnut branches in the court. Only I
I've lived here, Penned up inside this ghetto. But I have found what I love here.
It went away. way up high. would sing against a white stone. such, such a yellow
seven weeks I've lived here, penned up inside this ghetto.
And the white It went away I'm sure because it wished to kiss the world good-bye.
live in here. would sing against richly, brightly dazzlingly yellow.
butterflies don't live in here. For seven weeks
dandelions call to me And the white chestnut
It's carried lightly way up high.
good-bye. a white stone. Such, such a yellow
world It's carried lightly way up high.
the sun's tears Would sing against
a yellow if the sun's tears last, the very
Perhaps if the sun's tears would sing
The last, the very last, So richly.

THE
Butterfly

Pavel
Friedmann
June 4
1942

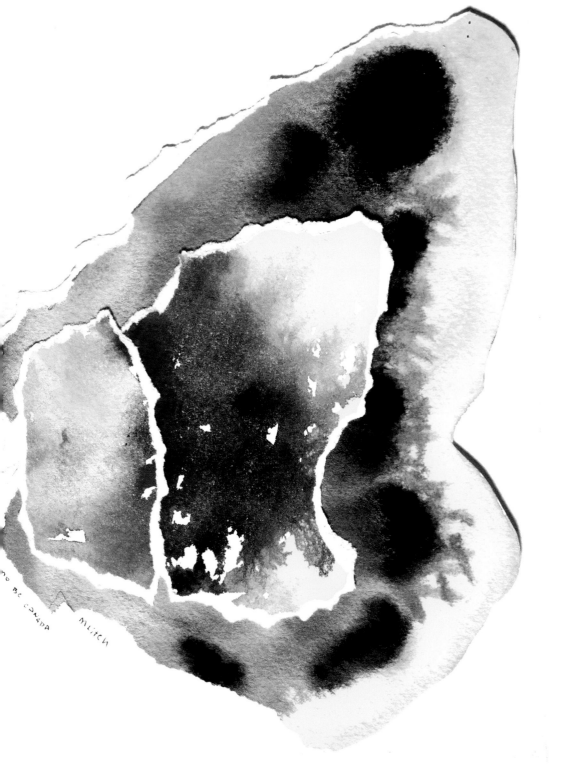

"Everyone has inside of him a piece of good news. The good news is that you don't know how great you can be! How much you can love! What you can accomplish! And what your potential is!"

~ ANNE FRANK

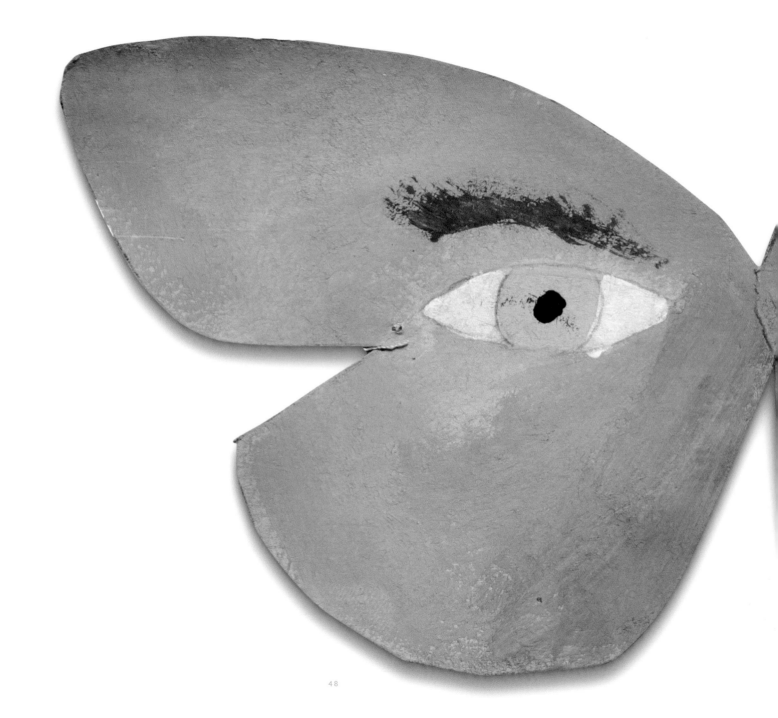

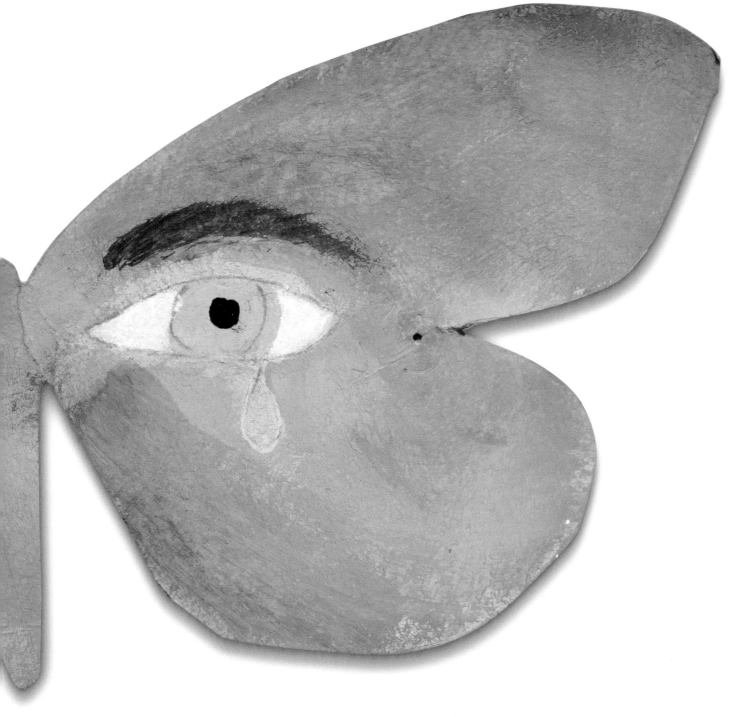

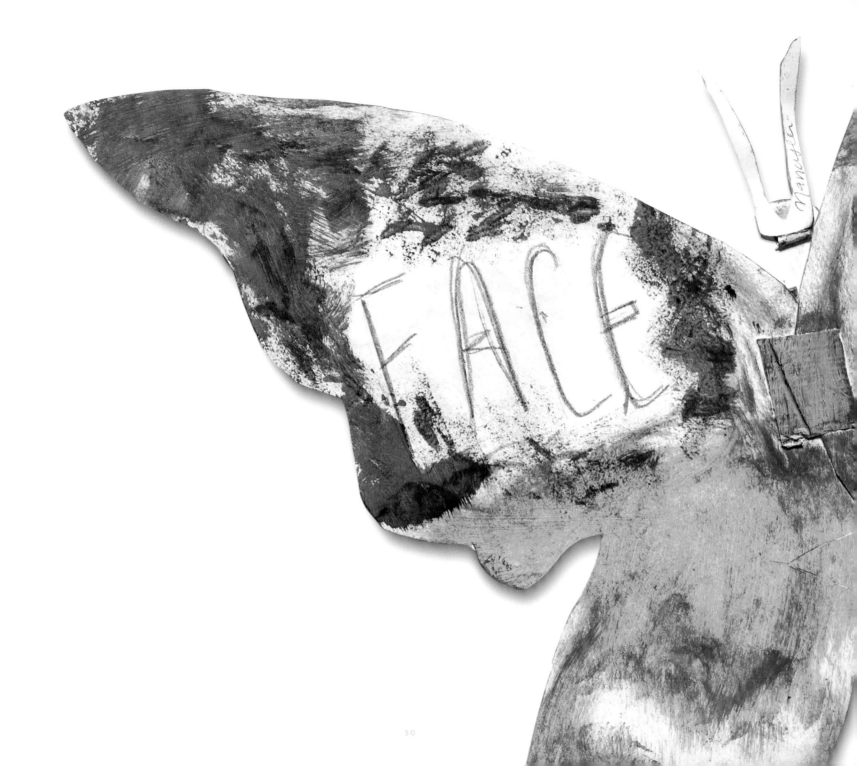

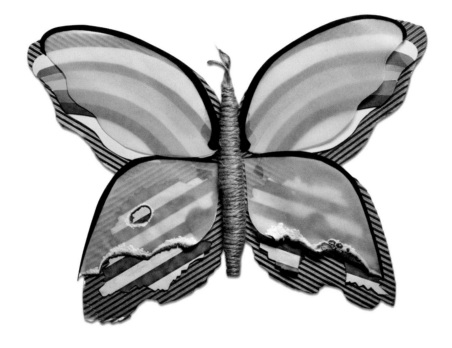

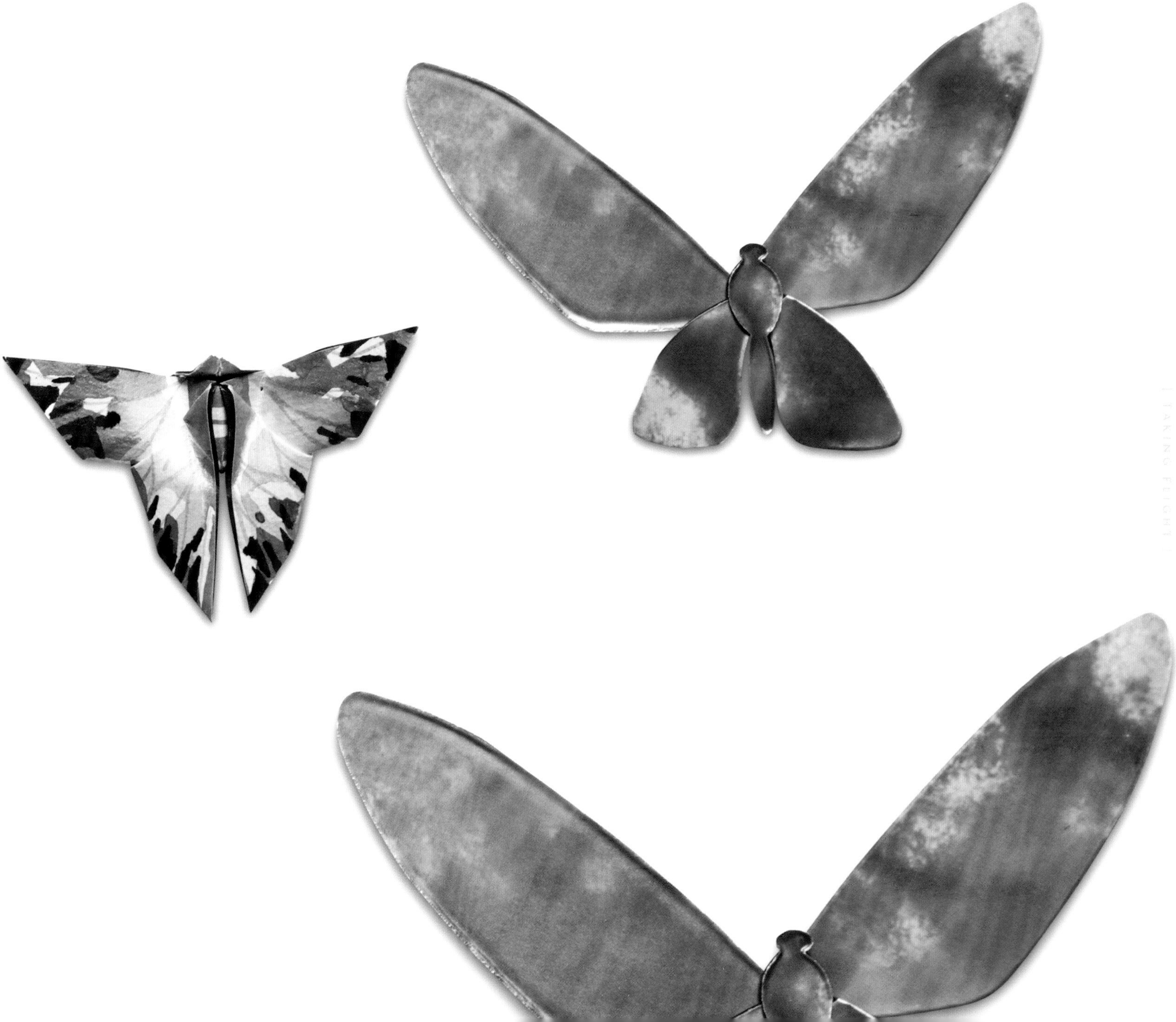

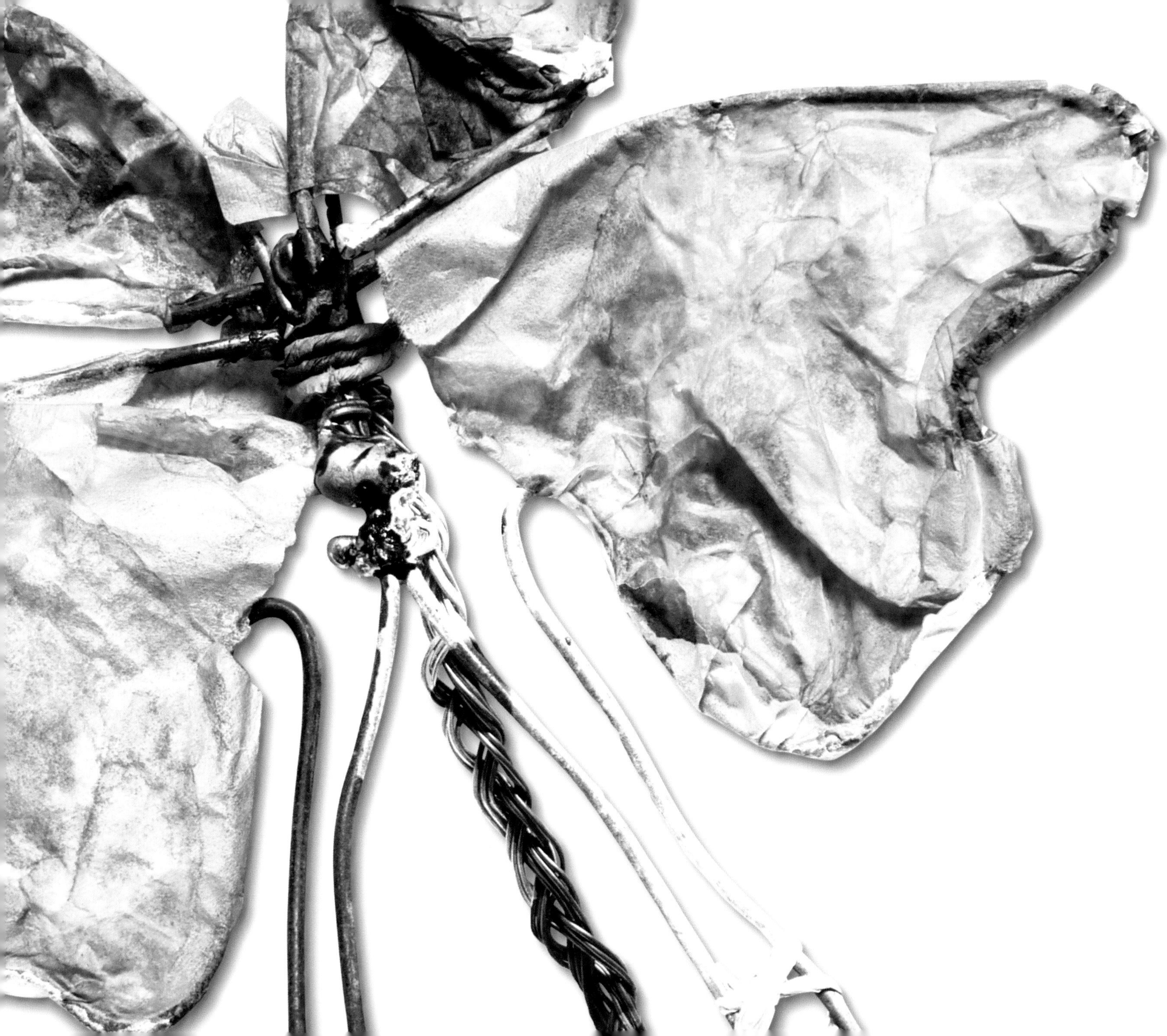

"All of humankind's understanding of reality and human nature, human destiny, the way we think about the world — all have been forever altered."

- CHAIM POTOK

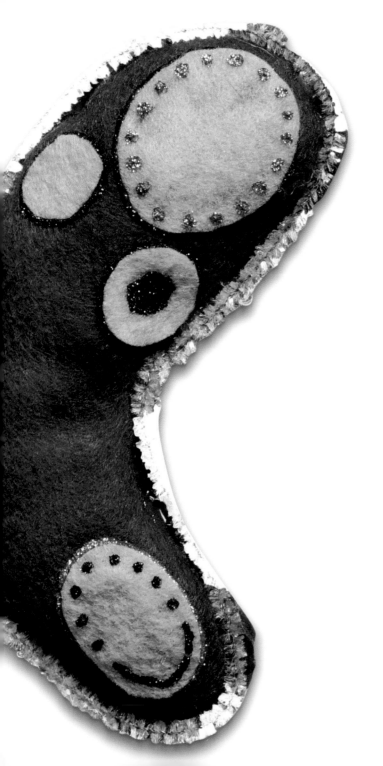

93

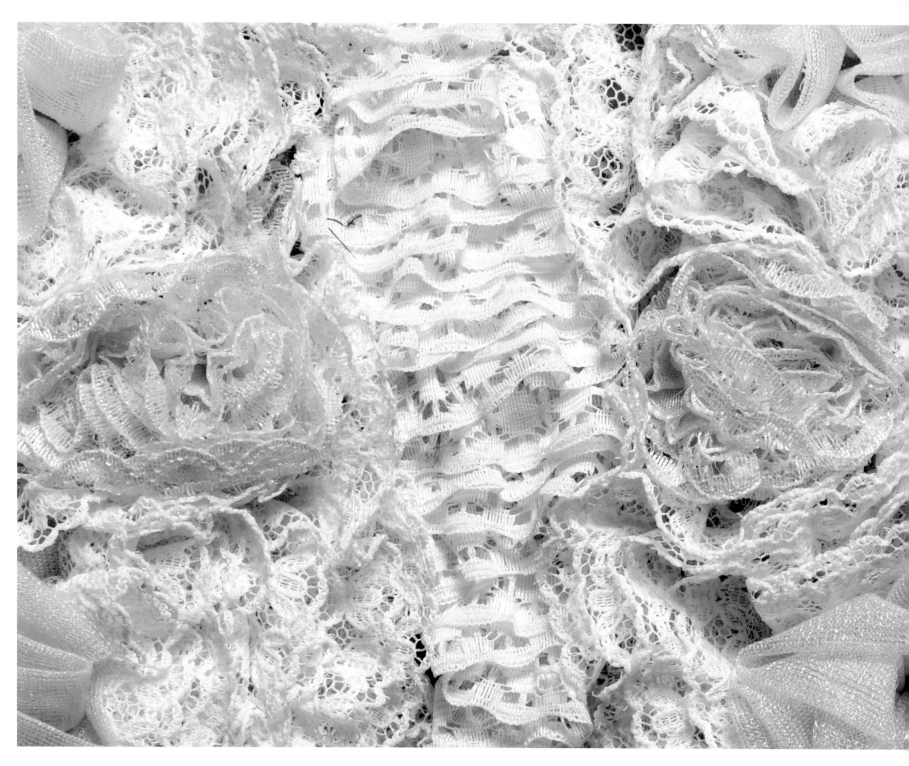

In Memory of my 3 first cousins from Kupishok, Lithuania

Jankelis, Pessa and baby Gesel,.

the children of my aunt Cipe Trapido Jachileviciene

In 1941, the 3 children, their mother, Cipe and their gandmother Roche were killed when the train taking them away from Kupishok to a place of safety was bombed. Jankelis was 9, Pese was 5 and the baby, Gesel, a year old.

Fay Trapido Morris

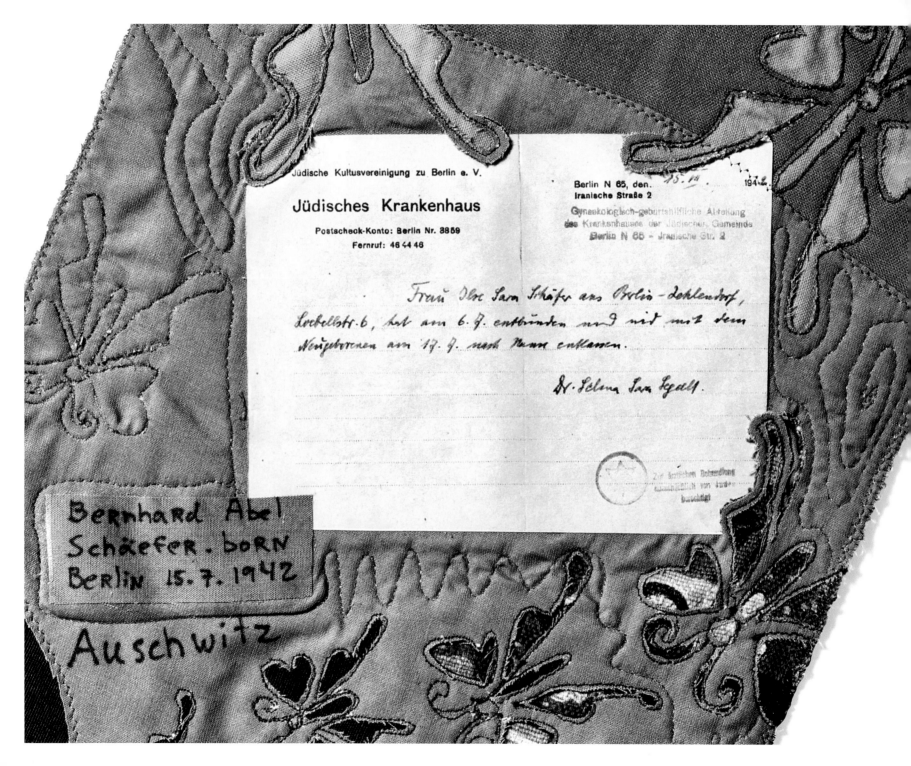

Jüdische Kultusvereinigung zu Berlin e. V.

Jüdisches Krankenhaus

Postscheck-Konto: Berlin Nr. 8859

Fernruf: 46 44 46

Berlin N 65, den. 15.14. 1942
Iranische Straße 2

Gynaekologisch-geburtshilfliche Abteilung
des Krankenhauses der Jüdischen Gemeinde
Berlin N 65 - Iranische Str. 2

Frau Ilse Sara Schäfer aus Berlin-Dahlendorf,
Loebellstr. 6, hat am 6.7. entbunden und ist mit dem
Neugeborenen am 17.7. nach Hause entlassen.

Dr. Selma Sara Egalt.

Zur ärztlichen Behandlung
ausschließlich von Juden
berechtigt

Bernhard Abel
Schäfer - born
Berlin 15.7.1942

Auschwitz

[TAKING FLIGHT]

113

ילדי ביה"ס קריית יערים
משתתפים במצגת הפרפרים

[TAKING FLIGHT]

117

Last night I
had a beautiful dream
I dreamed that I was at hom
I saw quite clearly our flat and
street. Now I am dissapointed and
out of sorts, because I awoke in a bunk
instead of my own bed. But maybe
this was some sort of omen of an
early end. Then there should be
permanent "lights out" all over Germany

Last night I had a beautiful dream. I dreamed that I was at home. I saw quite clearly our flat and street. Now I am dissapointed and out of sorts, because I awoke in a bunk instead of my own bed. But maybe this was some sort of omen of an early end. Then there should be permanent "lights out" all over Germany

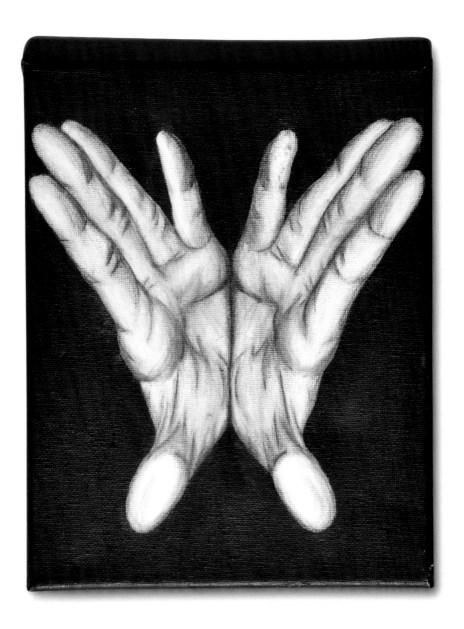

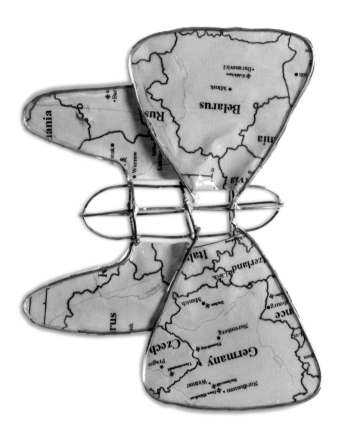

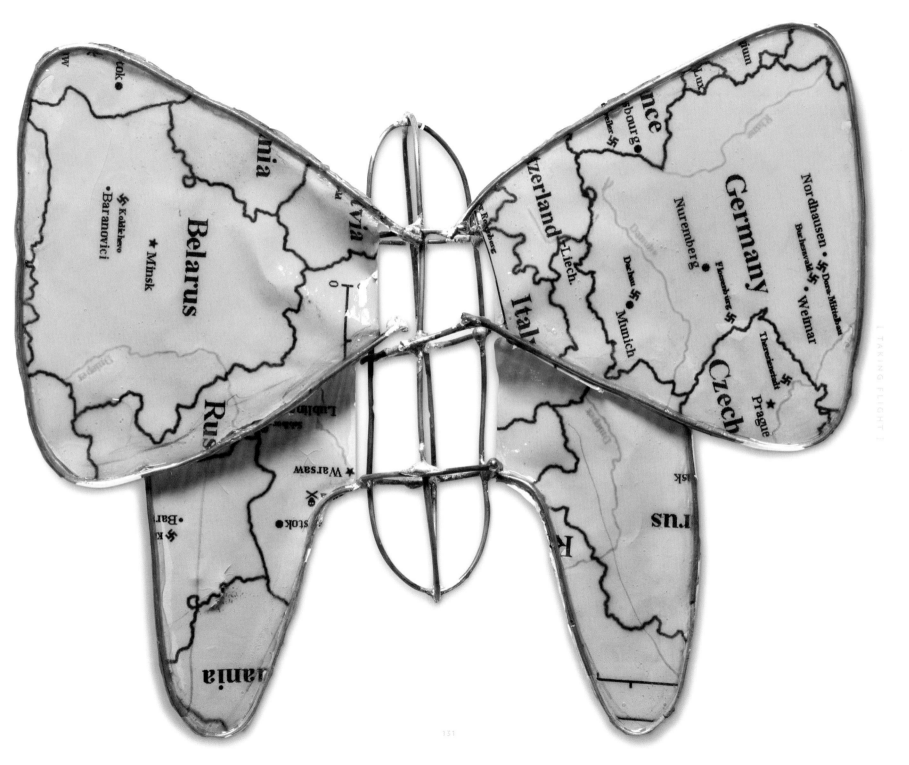

One after another,
Warm, fresh out of the oven,
Loaves of bread were carried to the poor
By young Adela Low.

Such a charitable kindness
Was carried in her gentle hands
Even the painter in the synagogue was seen
By young Adela Low.

When the awful war reached Poland,
That domed synagogue was destroyed,
But hope still remained
For young Adela Low.

They trusted a peasant to smuggle them away,
But the peasant's betrayal set their fate,
The Nazis shot eighteen – year – old
Young Adela Low.

Those loaves of bread were the last,
Not another would be carried
By young Adela Low.

-Liz Schleisman

Young Adela Low

Flour

"Those who forget the past are condemned to repeat it."

~ GEORGE SANTAYANA

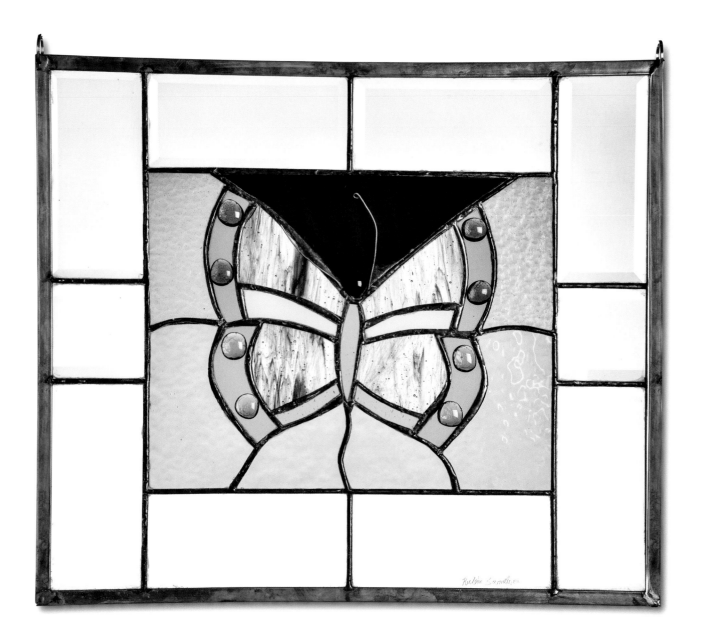

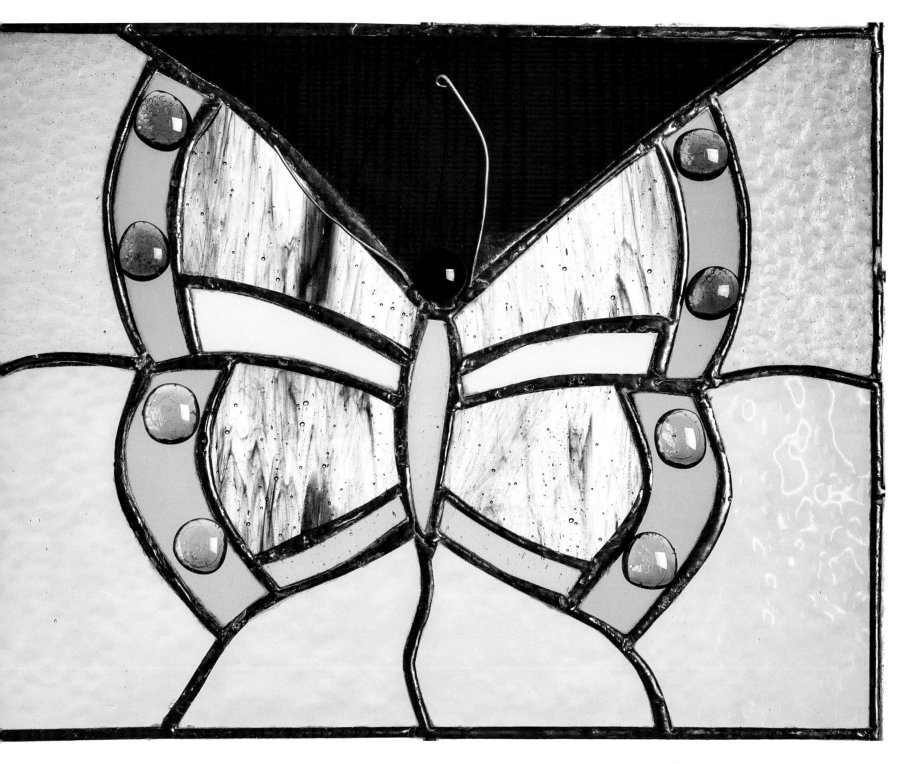

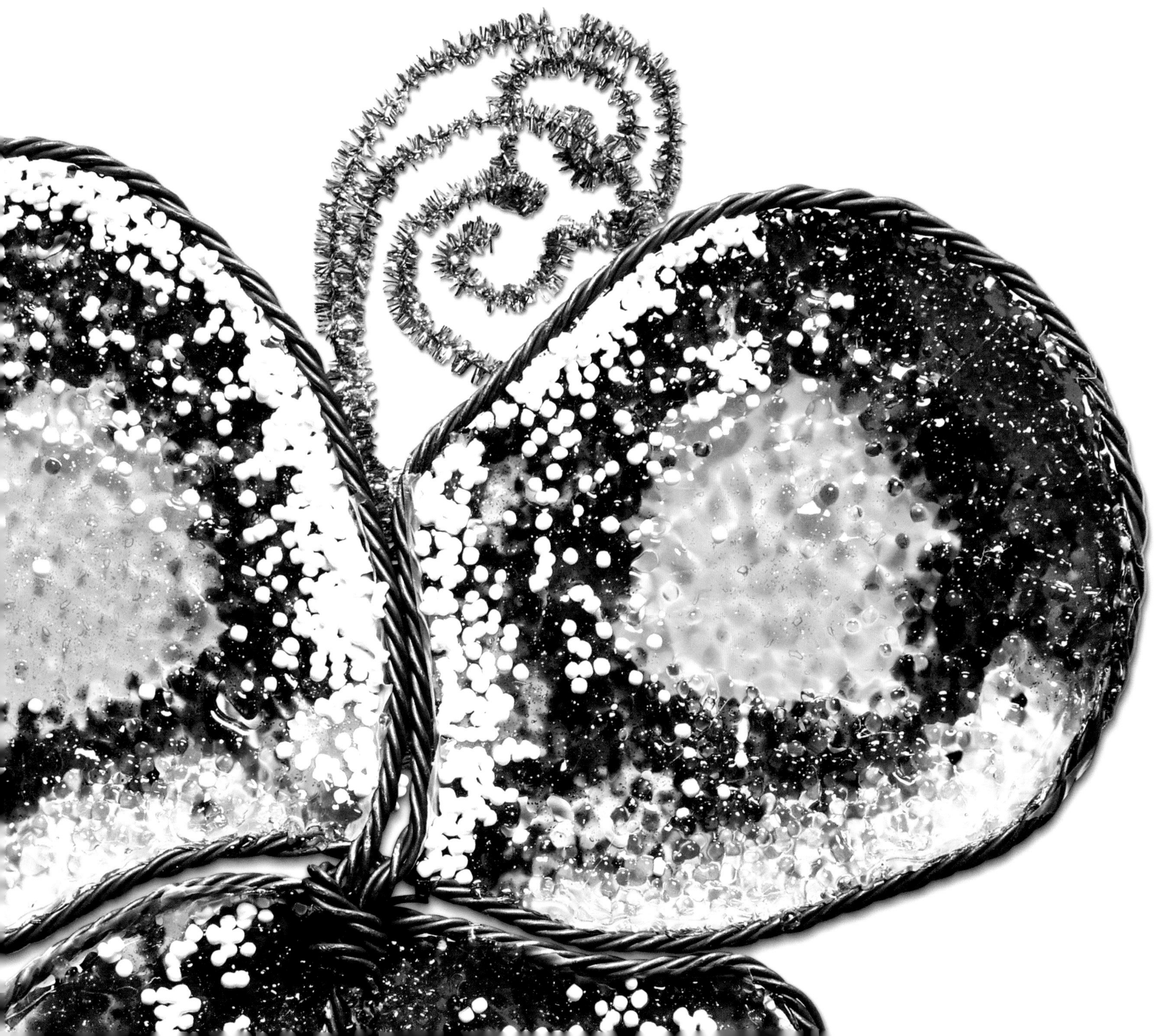

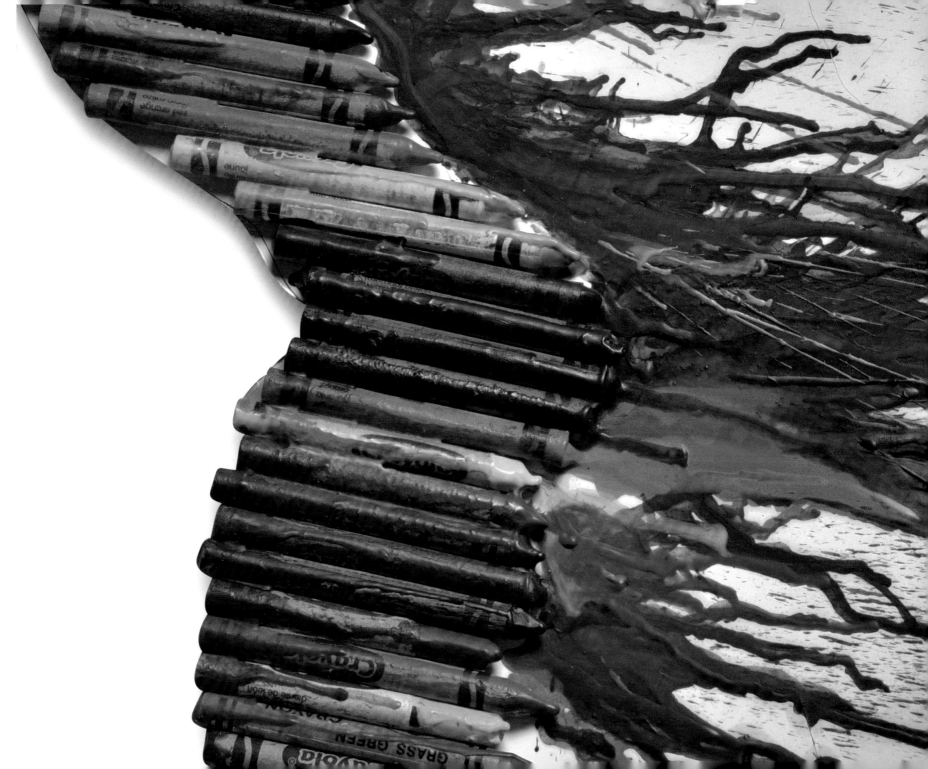

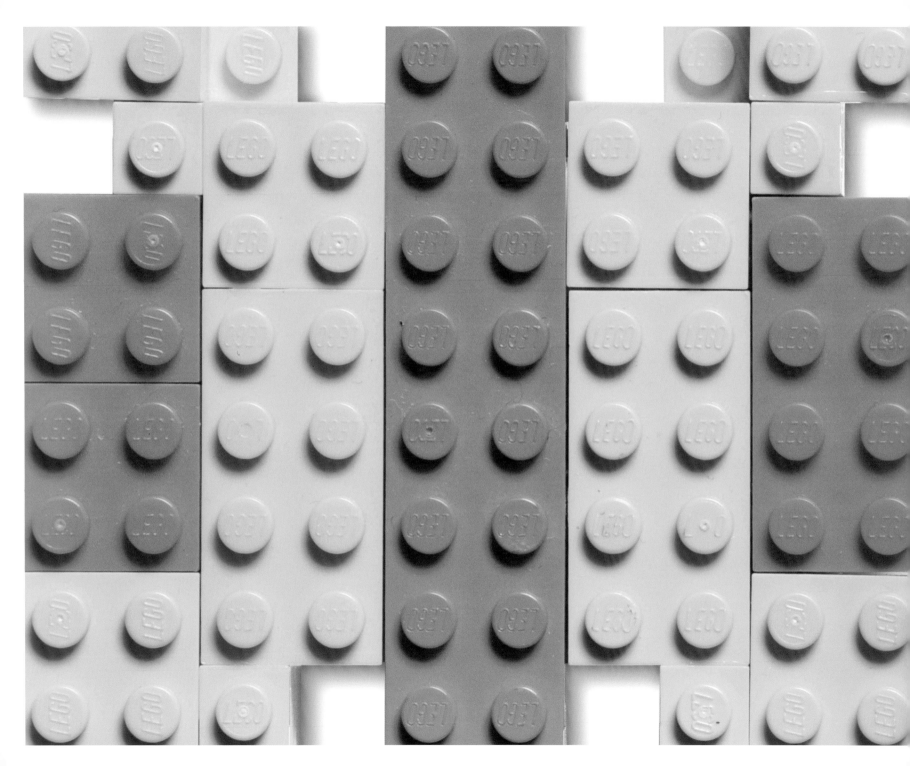

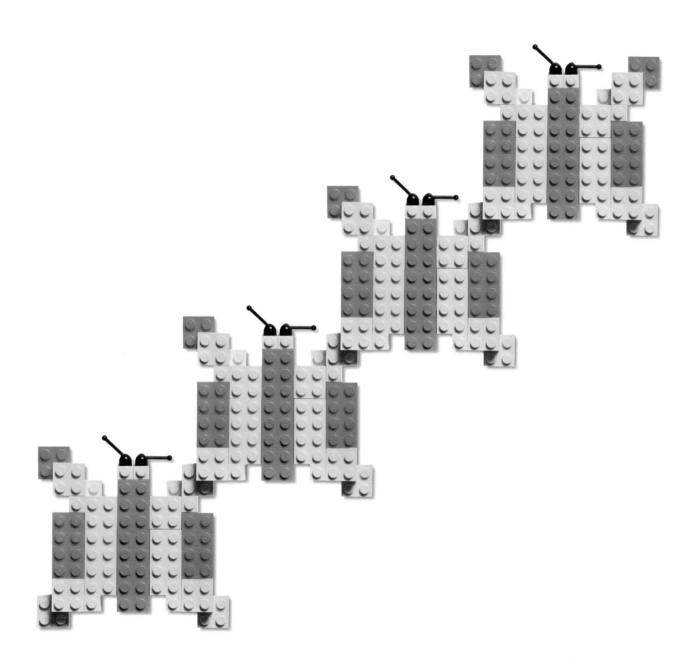

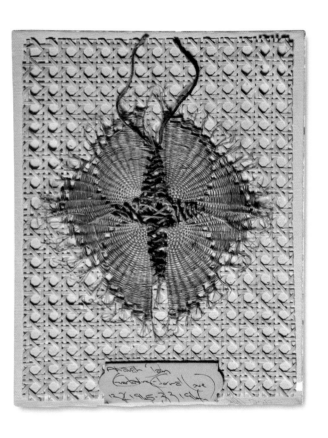

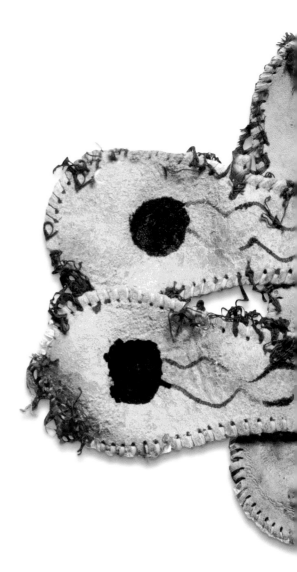

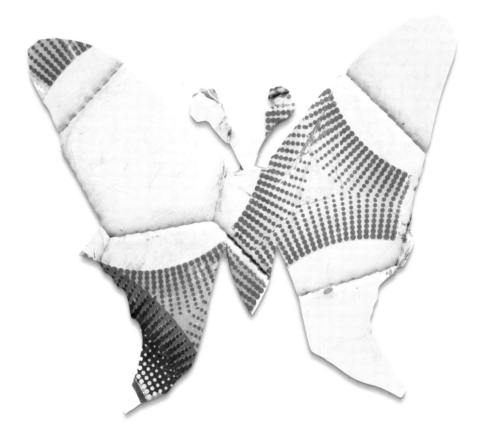

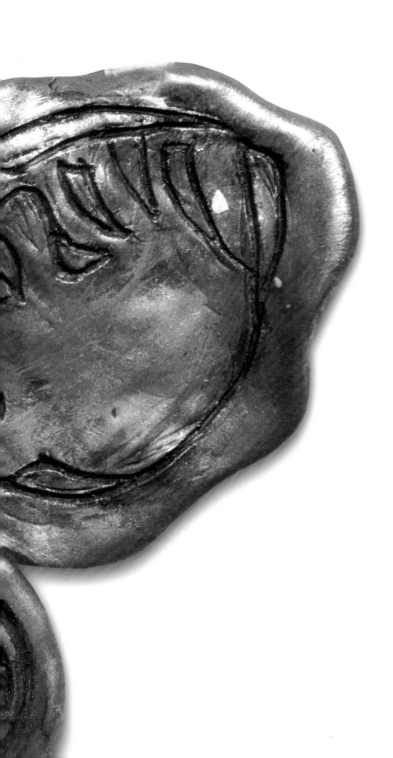

"Tell your children of it, and let your children tell their children, and their children another generation."

- JOEL 1:3

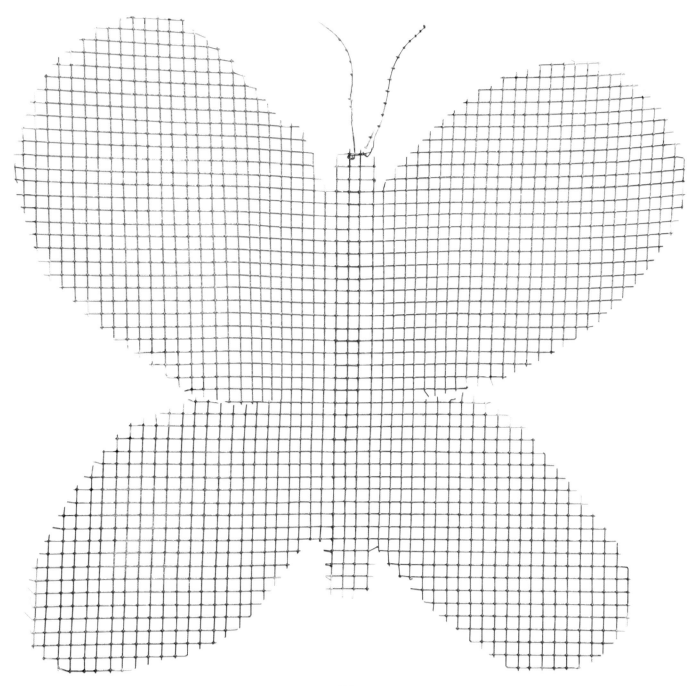

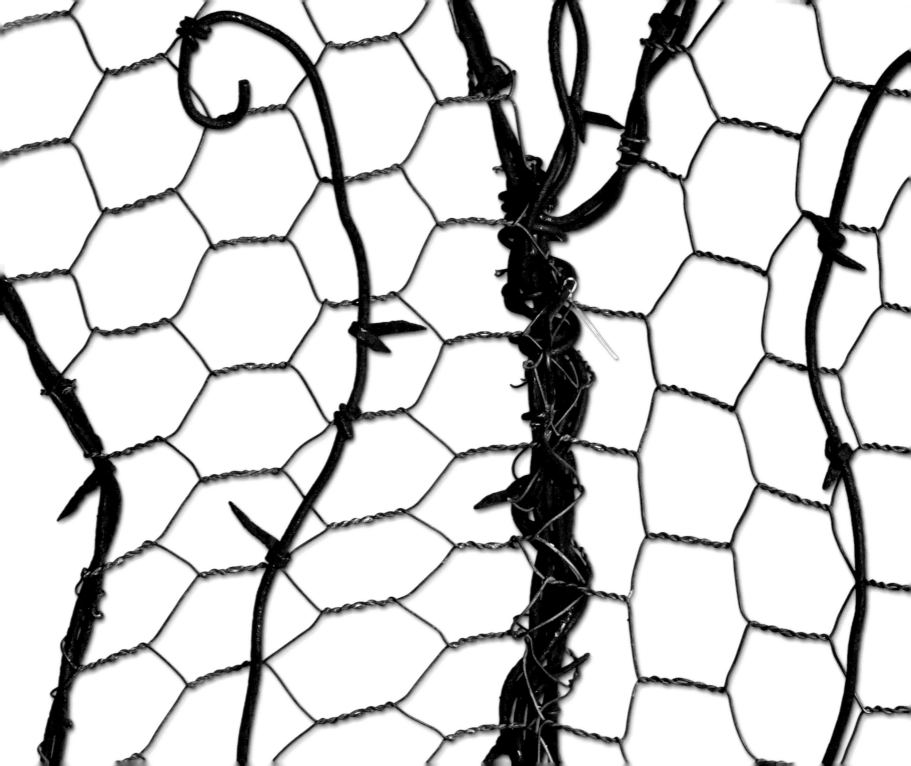

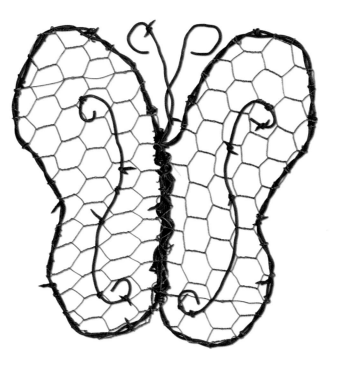

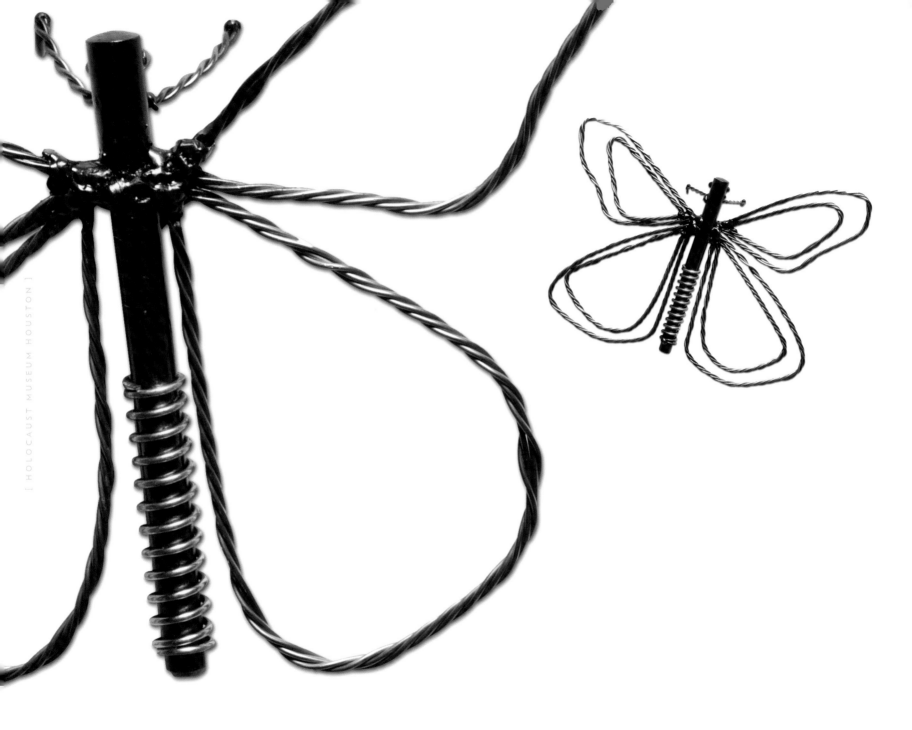

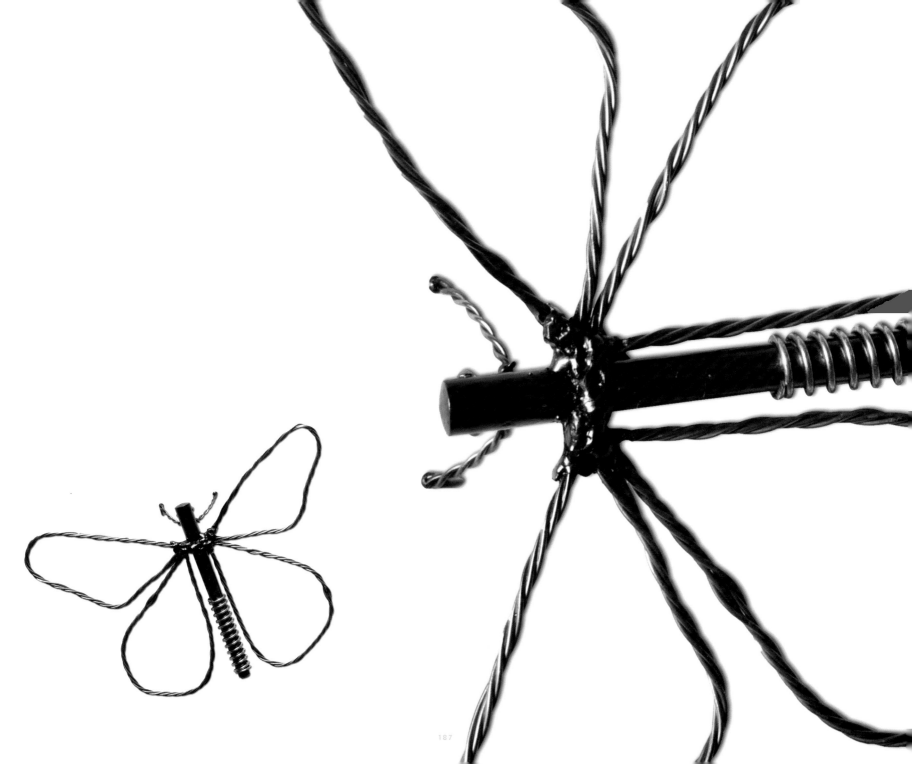

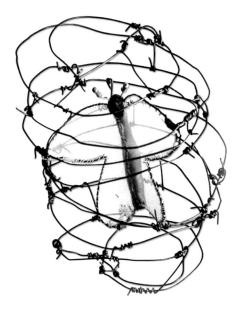

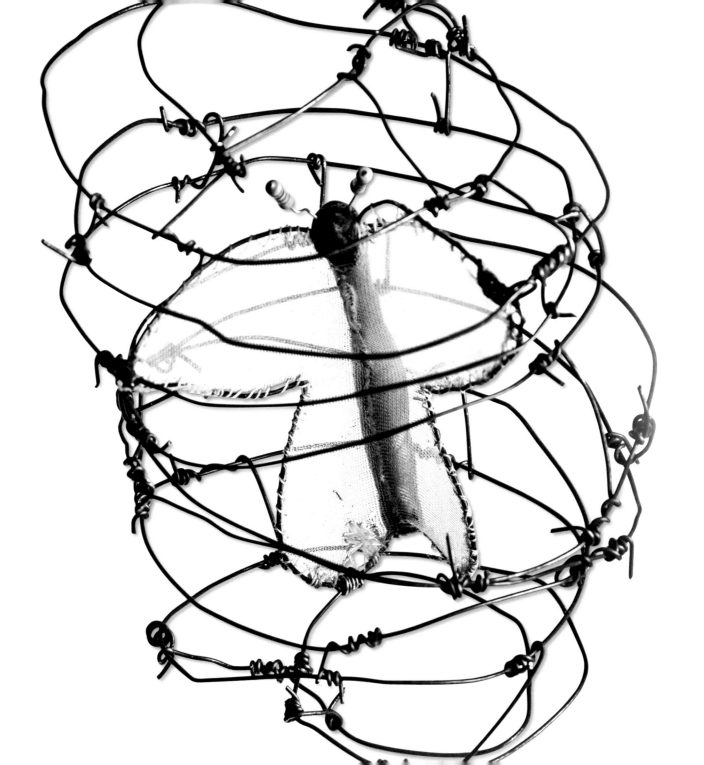

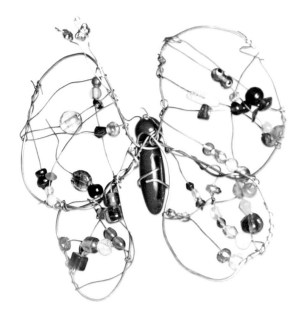

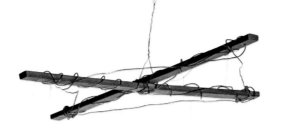

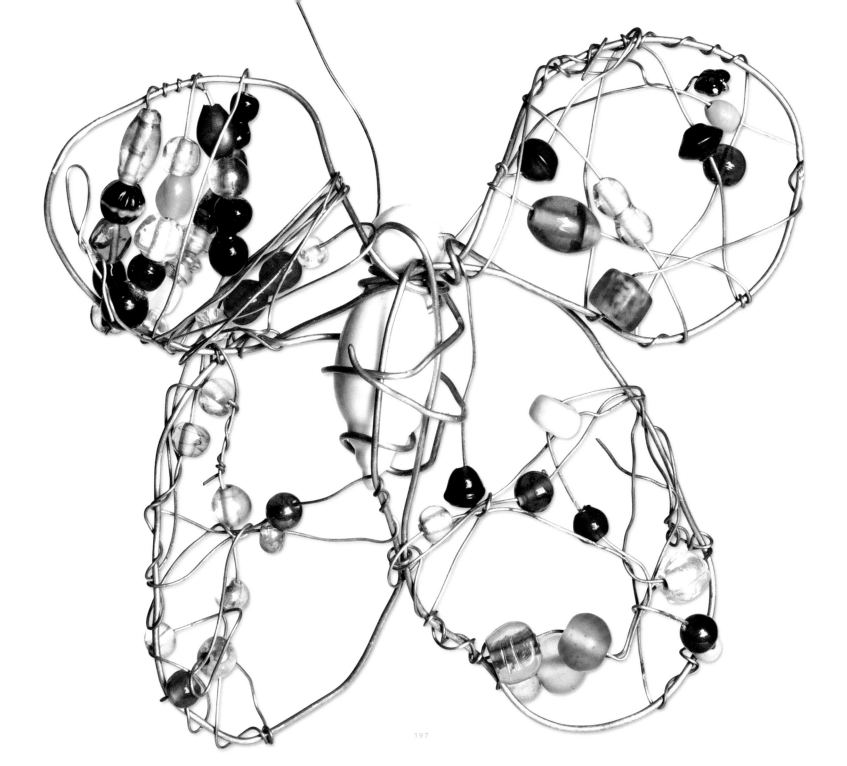

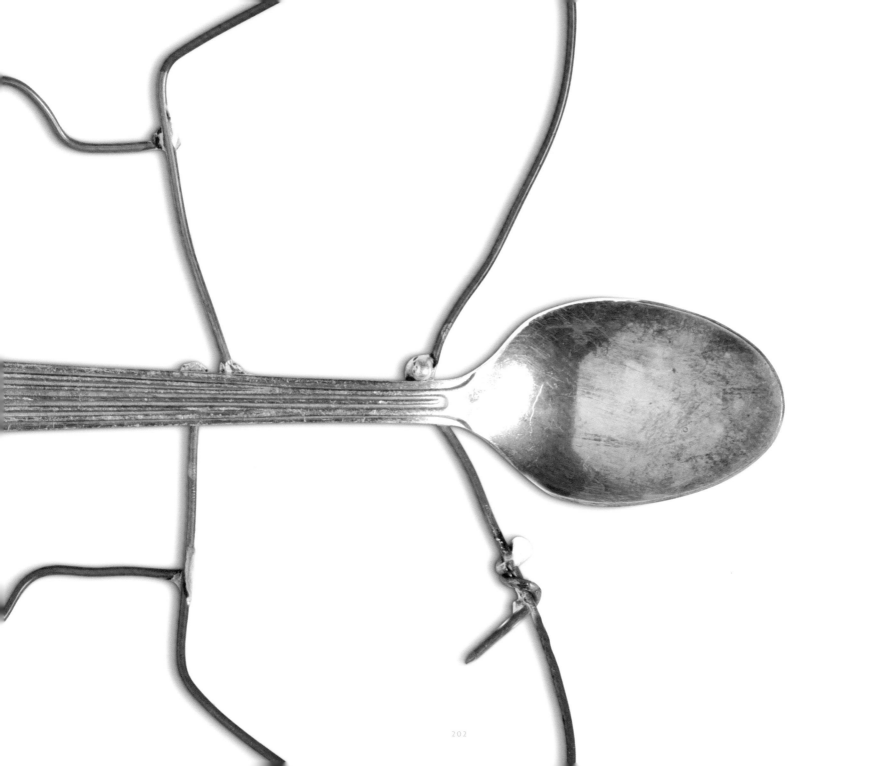

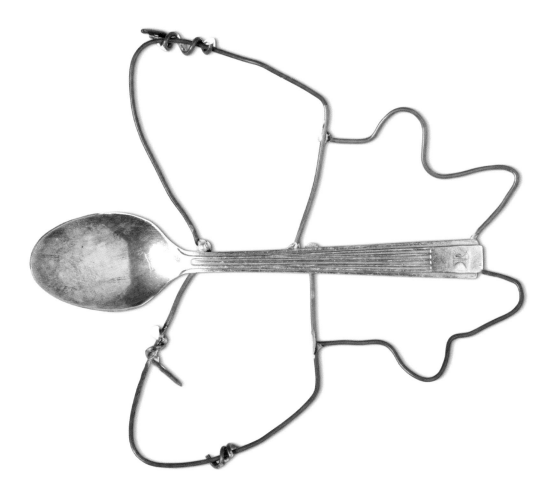

Coke®

Nutrition Facts

Serv. Size 1 Can

Amount Per Serving

Calories 140

% Daily Value*

Total Fat 0g 0%

Sodium 50mg 2%

Total Carb 39g 13%

Sugars 39g

Protein 0g

*Percent Daily Values
based on a 2,000 calorie

CARBONATED WATER, HIGH F
CORN SYRUP, CARA
PHOSPHORIC ACID, NA
FLAVORS, CAFFEINE.

CANNED UNDE
COCA-COLA CO
GA BY A

"For the dead and the living, we must bear witness."

- ELIE WIESEL